The Science Of
EQUINE FEEDING

THE PROPERLY NOURISHED HORSE IS A MAGNIFICENT DESIGN FOR SPEED AND ACTION, A SUPERBLY COORDINATED INTERPLAY OF BONE, MUSCLE AND NERVE. THE HORSE IS UNIQUE AND THIS VERY SPECIALIZATION DEMANDS SPECIALIZED FEEDING.

The Science Of
EQUINE
FEEDING

A Feeding Guide

BY

ELSIE HANAUER

South Brunswick and New York: A. S. Barnes and Company
London: Thomas Yoseloff Ltd

© 1973 by A. S. Barnes and Co., Inc.

A. S. Barnes and Co., Inc.
Cranbury, New Jersey 08512

Thomas Yoseloff Ltd
108 New Bond Street
London W1Y OQX, England

Library of Congress Cataloging in Publication Data

Hanauer, Elsie V
    The science of equine feeding.

    Bibliography: p.
    1. Horses—Feeding and feeds. I. Title.
SF285.5.H35   636.1'08'4   72-5190
ISBN 0-498-01183-6

By the same author

The Art of Whittling and Woodcarving
Bits of Knowledge
Creating with Leather
Dolls of the Indians
Guns of the Wild West
A Handbook of Crafts
Handbook of Wood Carving and Whittling
Horse Owner's Concise Guide
How to Make Egg Carton Figures
The Old West: People and Places

Printed in the United States of America

In Memory Of
Rocky

Contents

The Science Of
EQUINE
FEEDING

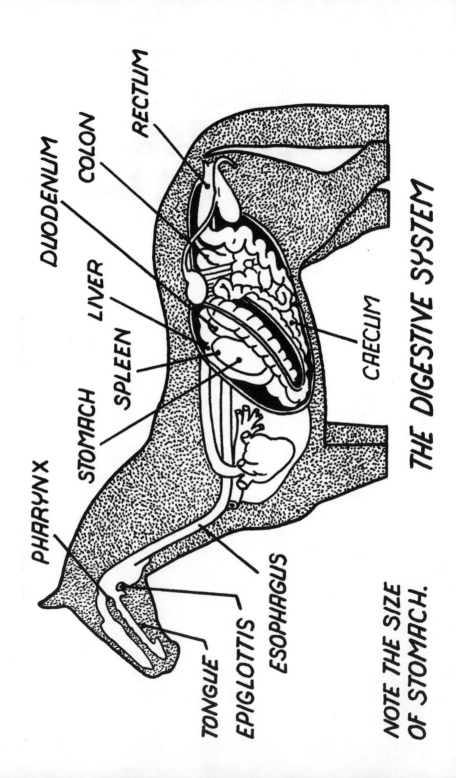

THE DIGESTIVE SYSTEM

NOTE THE SIZE OF STOMACH.

The Digestive System

THE MOUTH

The lips pick up food and it is then passed into the mouth by action of the tongue. It is masticated between the molar teeth and mixed with saliva, which moistens the mass for swallowing and as a digestive juice acts on the starches and sugars. The ball of masticated food is then forced past the soft palate into the pharynx by the base of the tongue.

THE PHARYNX

The muscular action of the pharynx forces the food into the esophagus. Once the food or water has entered the pharynx it cannot return to the mouth because of the traplike action of the soft palate. For this reason, a horse cannot breath through his mouth. Any food or water returned from the pharynx passes out through the nostrils.

THE ESOPHAGUS

The swallowed food is forced down the esophagus to the stomach by a progressive wave of constriction of the circular muscles of the organ. In the horse, this wave of constriction cannot move in the reverse direction and vomiting is impossible. The return of food or water through the nostrils is almost a certain indication that the horse is choked from a mass of food blocking the esophagus.

11

THE STOMACH

The esophageal and intestinal opening are close together and for this reason, water passes rather quickly through the stomach and small intestine to the first of the large intestines and the caecum. The food entering the stomach is arranged in layers, the end next to the small intestine filling first. No food leaves the stomach until it has been filled to about two-thirds of its capacity. As the horse eats, the partially digested food passes out into the small intestine in a continuous stream. As a result, up to three times the capacity of the stomach may pass out during a large meal. The emptying process slows up only when eating stops. The stomach is never completely empty unless food is withheld for one or two full days. The contents of the stomach are squeezed and pressed by the muscular activity of the organ, but the contents are never churned. The digestive juice, secreted by the walls of the stomach, contains the active digestive enzyme called pepsin which acts on the protein in the food. Some of the digested food is absorbed by the stomach, but as a whole, stomach digestion is partial preparatory digestion for more complete digestion in the intestines.

THE SMALL INTESTINE

The small intestine is arranged in a distinct U-shaped curve which prevents food from returning to the stomach once it has entered the intestine and also tends to close the opening into the intestine when the stomach is over-distended with food. The partially digested food in the small intestine is always quite fluid in character and passes rather rapidly through this part of the digestive tract.

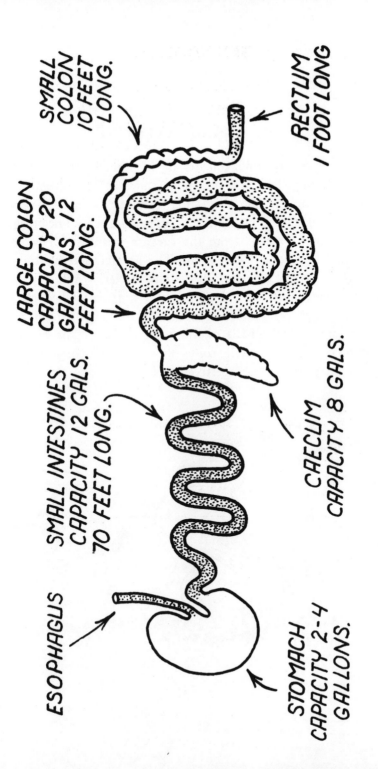

ESOPHAGUS

STOMACH
CAPACITY 2-4
GALLONS.

SMALL INTESTINES
CAPACITY 12 GALS.
70 FEET LONG.

CAECUM
CAPACITY 8 GALS.

LARGE COLON
CAPACITY 20
GALLONS. 12
FEET LONG.

SMALL
COLON
10 FEET
LONG.

RECTUM
1 FOOT LONG

SCHEMATIC DIAGRAM OF DIGESTIVE SYSTEM

Digestion is continued in the small intestine by the bile and pancreatic juice which is secreted by the liver and pancreas.

THE LARGE INTESTINE

The large intestine consists of five major components. They are the caecum, large colon, small colon, rectum and anus. In the caecum, digestion continues, some vitamin synthesis occurs and nutrients are absorbed. The large colon, which extends from the caecum to the small colon, is usually distended with food. The greater part of digestion of food by digestive juices and bacterial action takes place here. The absorption of most nutrients takes place in the large colon. The contents of the small colon are solid and here the balls of dung are formed. The rectum extends from the small colon to the anus, which is the terminal part of the digestive tract.

14

Food Requirements

The horse's body is composed of but a small group of the many elements found in nature. The elements found in his body in any quantity are carbon; hydrogen, one of the elements occurring in water; oxygen, found free in the air and water; and nitrogen, an air gas. In much smaller quantities there is found sulphur, iron, calcium, phosphorus, chlorine, fluorine, silica, manganese, potassium, sodium and copper. Aside from water, which comprises about 50% of the horse's body, the most important part of the animal's tissue is protein, which amounts to around 20% of the body weight. Protein is composed of carbon, hydrogen, oxygen, nitrogen and sulphur or phosphorus. The muscles, nerves and internal organs are largely protein. Fats, which are composed of carbon, hydrogen and oxygen, are the reserve food of the body. They form fatty tissues and occur mixed with other body tissues such as muscles. The amount of fat may vary from but a small amount to nearly 50% of the body weight. Carbohydrates, which are also made up of carbon, hydrogen and oxygen, form a small part of the horse's body. The mineral elements, occurring mostly in bone, account for over 4% of the body weight.

The horse requires food for growth, repair of worn-out body tissue, fuel to maintain body temperature, energy for the vital body functions of the heart, lungs and digestion, and energy for the production of movement or external work.

Protein is required for body growth and repair of worn-out tissues and minerals are required for the bones. Carbohydrates and fats are needed for the production of heat and energy or to be stored as fat for an energy-food reserve.

The horse's body may be compared to a gasoline engine. For fuel the horse uses food, and by his process of digestion, breaks down the proteins, carbohydrates and fats and absorbs them into the body, where they are used to repair any worn-out tissues and to produce heat and muscle energy. Like the exhaust gases of an engine, the indigestible matter and body waste products are thrown off. Heat and energy are produced within the body by a process of oxidation. Like the engine, the more work the body does the less efficient it becomes, the more fuel it requires, and the greater is the wear and repair needed. Proportionally, the demand of food for repairs increases more rapidly than the demand of fuel for energy. In any food a definite ratio exists between the nutritive value of the tissue-building proteins and the heat- and energy-producing carbohydrates and fats. This is known as the nutritive ratio. The nutritive ratio for horses should be between 1 and 11 for idle horses, and between 1 and 7 for hard-working animals.

GOOD QUALITY OATS AND HAY BOTH CONTAIN 12% PROTEIN. POOR QUALITY OATS AND HAY MAY CONTAIN AS LITTLE AS 9% PROTEIN. IF FEEDING LOW PROTEIN OATS AND HAY, MORE PROTEIN MAY BE ADDED TO THE RATION IN THE FORM OF DEHY-DRATED ALFALFA PELLETS OR SOYBEAN MEAL.

Food Value

The food value of any feed is probably best measured in terms of the amount and proportion of the disgestible nutrients it supplies; however, its palatability, bulk, mineral content, vitamin content and net energy value are factors to also be considered. A table given below shows the feeding values of the most common horse feeds.

CONCENTRATE	DRY MATTER	DIG. PROTEIN	TOTAL DIG. NUTRIENTS	NUTRITIVE RATIO
OATS	91.1	9.4	71.5	6.6
DENT CORN	88.5	7.4	83.7	10.3
WHEAT BRAN	90.6	13.1	70.2	4.4
BARLEY	90.4	9.3	78.7	7.5
LINSEED MEAL	91.3	30.6	78.2	1.6
COTTONSEED MEAL	39.5	35.0	75.5	1.2
DRY ROUGHAGE				
ALFALFA	90.4	10.6	50.3	3.7
CLOVER	88.2	7.0	51.9	6.4
TIMOTHY	88.7	2.9	46.9	15.2
OAT HAY	88.0	4.5	46.3	9.3
GRASS HAY	89.0	3.5	51.7	13.8
GREEN ROUGHAGE				
ALFALFA	25.4	3.4	14.7	3.3
MIXED GRASS	29.7	3.6	20.2	4.6
CARROTS	11.9	0.8	9.6	11.0

CLOSELY STABLED HORSES AND THOSE CONFINED TO SMALL PENS WILL OFTEN CHEW WOOD AND EVEN EAT MANURE. THESE UNDESIRABLE HABITS ARE NOT NECESSARILY A SIGN OF THEIR LACKING SOMETHING IN THE DIET. IN MOST CASES SUCH ANIMALS ARE BORED. THIS IS THEIR WAY OF RELAXING AND THROW-BACK TO THE STRONG GRAZING INSTINCT.

Vitamins

Vitamins are essential for the proper growth and health of horses. They do not themselves contribute to the energy supply of the body, but facilitate utilization of the proteins, carbohydrates, fats and minerals.

Vitamin A

Vitamin A is needed by the digestive, respiratory and reproductive systems of all horses, but it is especially important for normal growth in foals. This particular vitamin does not actually exist in plants, but the green leaves of plants do contain carotene which is changed into Vitamin A by action of the horse's small intestine and liver.

The leaves of green plants are said to contain more carotene than the stems. For example, the leaves of alfalfa contain six times more carotene than the stems. Green roughage contains considerable carotene during its early growth but as it becomes older, the amount of carotene decreases. Once the roughage has become dry or weathered, it contains so little carotene that horses fed on it for long periods may suffer from Vitamin A deficiency.

Symptoms of Vitamin A deficiency are normally a picky appetite, poor hoof development and night blindness. A lack of Vitamin A may also affect the fertility of both mares and stallions.

Vitamin D

Vitamin D is required for the development of strong bones

and teeth. Mature horses, except pregnant mares, require much less of this vitamin than young foals. Sunlight is the source of Vitamin D and most horses exposed to considerable sunlight during the growing season will receive an ample supply of this vitamin.

Symptoms of Vitamin D deficiency are mainly rickets and retared growth in young horses. Pregnant mares who have been deprived of ample sunlight may produce weak foals or those born with malformations.

Vitamin E

Vitamin E aids in the development and maintenance of muscle and is equally important in the reproductive qualities of the horse. This vitamin is normally abundant in green roughage and supplements are rarely required.

THE B-COMPLEX VITAMINS

There are ten known B-Complex Vitamins and the normal horse feeds contain most of them in adequate amounts. Good quality green roughages contain these important vitamins. Vitamin B-12 must normally be added to horse feeds.

Thiamine

Thiamine, or B-1 is not only required for metabolism or carbohydrates, but it also promotes a good appetite and is very beneficial for reproduction. Thiamine is normally found in regular horse feeds and supplements are rarely required.

Symptoms of Thiamine deficiency are normally a loss of appetite and weight. Continued deficiency of this vitamin may result in poor coordination and nervousness.

Riboflavin

Riboflavin, or Vitamin B-2, is very essential in the oxidation of living cells and if the horse is fed adequate amounts of good quality leafy roughage, there is little worry of Riboflavin deficiency.

Symptoms of Riboflavin deficiency are first noticed by a picky appetite. In young animals there is normally a reduction in the growth rate.

Niacin

Niacin is essential to the metabolism of the carbohydrates and protein. This B-Complex vitamin is widely found in regular horse feeds and supplements are not normally needed.

Vitamin B-12

Vitamin B-12 improves the horse's appetite, increases utilization of foods, promotes growth in young horses and also is important in normal reproduction.

Pantothenic Acid

Pantothenic acid is required for the life process and it is normally supplied in ample amounts when the horse is fed a good quality alfalfa hay or green grass. Wheat bran also contains Pantothenic acid.

Choline

Choline builds and maintains the cell structures and the metabolism of fat in the liver. Choline is normally available in sufficient amounts in regular horse feeds.

Vitamin C

Vitamin C is required by horses in small amounts and adequate amounts are normally furnished in regular horse feeds.

Vitamin K

Vitamin K is very important as it preserves the clotting power of blood and helps to reduce bleeding from wounds. This vitamin is found in green roughage, especially alfalfa.

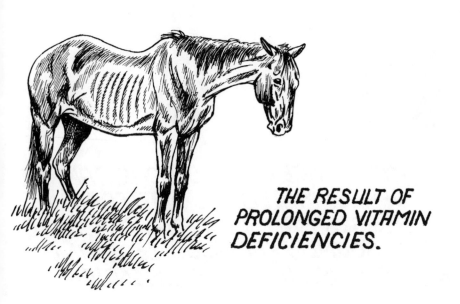

THE RESULT OF PROLONGED VITAMIN DEFICIENCIES.

GOOD BONE IS IMPORTANT

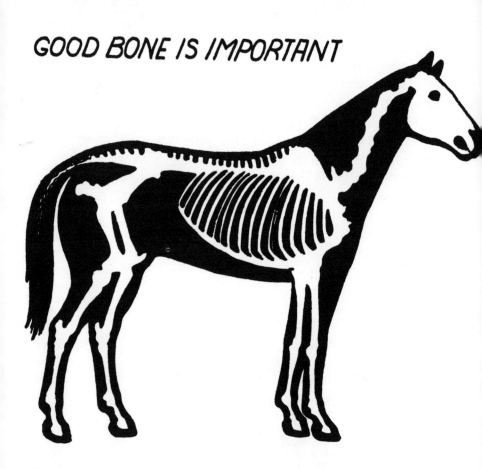

THE IMPORTANCE OF GOOD BONE CANNOT BE OVERESTIMATED. NO MATTER WHAT THE HORSE'S BREED OR PURPOSE, GOOD BONE, SOUND FEET, GOOD LEGS AND WELL-SPRUNG RIBS ARE ESSENTIAL.

CALCIUM, PHOSPHORUS AND VITAMIN D ARE THE "BIG 3" OF BONE FORMATION.

Minerals

The most critical needs for minerals are during growth, reproduction, lactation and heavy exercise. Minerals are most likely to be deficient in normal horse rations because the soils of some areas are mineral-deficient, and pastures, hays and grains from these soils are likewise mineral-deficient.

Salt

Salt is composed of chlorine and sodium, which help to transfer the nutrients to the cells and remove any waste materials. While sodium is very important in making bile, which aids digestion of fats and the carbohydrates, chlorine is required in the gastric juices for the digestion of protein. Deficiency of salt may lead to a rough coat, depraved appetite and a growth reduction in young horses.

Calcium

Calcium is needed by the horse to develop strong bones. Young horses deprived of calcium may develop rickets, while older animals may suffer from a bone condition known as Osteomalacia.

Phosphorous

Phosphorous is also required for developing strong bones and a proper ratio of phosphorous and calcium must be maintained.

Iodine

Iodine is required by the horse's thyroid gland. This mineral is deficient in some areas of the country and must therefore be supplemented. A lack of iodine in the diet may cause mares to have weak or stillborn foals.

Iron

Iron is needed to make hemoglobin and is also essential to enzyme systems. Regular horse feeds contain enough iron for the average horse.

Cobalt

Cobalt is needed by the bacteria which are important in the digestion of food and is also essential in the synthesis of the B-Complex vitamins.

Copper

Copper serves much the same purposes in the horse as iron.

Sulfur

Sulfur is an essential part of many proteins, vitamins and compounds required for the horse's vital processes. Under normal conditions, sulfur is required only in small amounts.

Manganese, Magnesium and Potassium

Manganese, magnesium and potassium are required only in small amounts by the horse and a sufficient supply is normally found in regular horse feeds.

A TRACE MINERAL STOC
BLOCK IS, IN MOST CASES,
A SIMPLE, BUT EFFECTIVE
AND INEXPENSIVE METHOD
OF SUPPLEMENTING NEEDED
MINERALS.

A STANDARD TYPE TRACE
MINERAL BLOC IS DE-
SCRIBED BELOW. SMALLER
BLOCS ARE AVAILABLE.

TRACE MINERAL BLOC

SALT	maximum	97.00%
SALT	minimum	95.00%
ZINC (Zn)	minimum	0.600%
MANGANESE (Mn)	minimum	0.300%
IRON (Fe)	minimum	0.230%
COPPER (Cu)	minimum	0.033%
IODINE (I)	minimum	0.012%
COBALT (Co)	minimum	0.012%

INGREDIENTS:

SALT, ZINC OXIDE, MANGANOUS OXIDE, FERROUS
CARBONATE, COPPER OXIDE, CALCIUM IODATE,
COBALT OXIDE, WHITE MINERAL OIL, CANE
MOLASSES AND RED IRON OXIDE.

50 LBS. NET WT.

27

A HORSE THAT IS SLIGHTLY UNDER HIS NORMAL WEIGHT BECAUSE OF TOO LITTLE GRAIN, BUT WITH PLENTY OF VITAMINS AND MINERALS IN HIS SYSTEM, IS IN BETTER PHYSICAL CONDITION THAN A HORSE WITH NORMAL WEIGHT FROM AN ABUNDANCE OF GRAIN, BUT WHOSE SYSTEM IS LACKING IN VITAMINS AND MINERALS.

Water

Water is important for dissolving nutrients and also reacts with chemical compounds, breaking down complex food substances. Combined with water, these substances are then able to be absorbed and utilized. Water is also required for temperature control. When the horse becomes overheated, evaporation cools him. Water actually absorbs heat and the watery tissues of the horse's body stabilize the body temperature.

Plenty of fresh water is essential to a horse's health. Under normal conditions, the average horse will consume around 10 gallons of water a day, but during hot, dry weather or after hard exercise he will consume more. During cold weather the horse will naturally drink less water and often may not consume enough for body requirements. Salt added to the daily grain ration will usually encourage a horse to drink more water. All water containers or stock tanks should be kept clean and filled with fresh water. To be sure of an adequate water supply, it is wise to check and fill at each feeding.

Factors Influencing Feeding

Quantity

Insufficient food, particularly bulky food, causes loss of condition and general debility, and predisposes a horse to devastating diseases. Food in excess of body needs is harmful as it overtaxes the digestive organs and may cause diarrhea due to irritation or colic due to constipation.

Combination of Feeds

Horses cannot thrive on concentrated foods. Bulk is absolutely essential if the digestive tract is to be properly distended and digestion unimpaired. Excessive amounts of proteins, fats or carbohydrates decrease the digestibility of the whole ration.

Water

The nutrients of the food must be solution before they can be absorbed. Sweating can greatly deplete the water content of the body tissues. To compensate for this loss, water is drawn from the digestive tract. A deficiency of water in the digestive tract not only affects digestion, but is also liable to affect the general health of the horse by causing such diseases as debility and colic.

THE FREQUENCY AND DISTRIBUTION OF FOOD
HAS A GREAT DEAL TO DO WITH ITS UTI-
LIZATION AND THE CONDITION OF THE HORSE.
BECAUSE A DIGESTIVE TRACT DISTENDED
WITH HAY IS A HINDRANCE IN WORK, IT IS
BEST TO FEED MOST OF THE HAY AT NIGHT.
THE COMMON PRACTICE IS TO FEED ONE-
FOURTH OF THE DAILY HAY ALLOWANCE
AT EACH OF THE MORNING AND NOON FEED-
INGS, AND THE REMAINING HALF AT NIGHT
WHEN THE HORSE HAS PLENTY OF TIME IN
WHICH TO EAT LEISURELY.

Principles Of Feeding

WATER BEFORE FEEDING

Horses drink very rapidly and the water passes quickly through both the stomach and small intestines into the caecum. Such a stream passing through a full stomach washes a considerable portion of the contents into the bowels. If the horse has just finished his meal, the food is only partially mixed with gastric juices and digestion is incomplete. Therefore there is a loss of nourishment and indigestion or colic may result.

When water is constantly available to the horse he will normally not drink enough at one time to do any harm, but beware of the exceptions to the rule. For these animals it is best to water before feeding and again one hour after the meal.

FEED IN SMALL QUANTITIES

Considering his size and the amount of food consumed, the stomach of the horse is relatively small. In his natural state the horse was a slow, but more or less a constant eater and did not require a stomach of great storage capacity. The maximum capacity of the stomach is about four gallons, but it functions more efficiently when it contains only two and one half gallons. These facts should have a decided influence on the methods of horse feeding. The small size of the stomach makes it imperative that food be given in small amounts and at relatively frequent intervals. Overloading a horse's stomach not only lowers its efficiency as a digestive organ but, by pressure against the diaphragm, makes breathing difficult.

DO NOT WORK HARD AFTER A MEAL

Immediately after a meal, the stomach and bowels are more distended, containing more food and water. As a result they require more space than prior to feeding. This extra space is gained by a slight filling out of the abdomen and by the stomach bulging forward against the diaphragm. The size of the thoracic cavity is then reduced and the lungs are prevented from expanding to their fullest. With exercise, the horse therefore has difficulty in obtaining sufficient fresh air and labored breathing is the result.

Another danger of working the horse hard immediately after a meal is the interference with digestion. Digestion is accompanied by increased muscular activity of the bowels, increased blood supply to the digestive tract and increased flow of secretions. Hard work will divert blood to other channels, tire the intestinal muscles and reduce secretions. This retarded digestion can result in serious disorders of the digestive tract and it always results in loss of food nourishment.

DO NOT FEED AN EXHAUSTED HORSE

The digestive organs of a tired horse are just as tired as the rest of his body. The muscular layers of the stomach and intestines are tired, the nervous energy is depleted and the glands of secretion will not function normally because the bulk of blood is still in body muscles.

Small amounts of water may be given an exhausted horse

EXHAUSTED HORSES SHOULD BE RESTED BEFORE FEEDING.

at frequent intervals, but grain and any large amount of hay should be withheld for about two hours. Failure to observe this principle could result in serious colic, laminitis or both.

FEED HAY BEFORE GRAIN

Hay fed before feeding grain stimulates an increased flow of saliva and gastric juices, and as the food tends to leave the stomach in the order of its receipt, the grain will be held longer in the stomach and undergo more complete digestion.

DO NOT OVERFEED A HORSE

Overfeeding often occurs in today's horses and it is the most common cause of such diseases as colic, laminitis, Azoturia and lymphangitis. Most of the harm is caused by feeding too much grain to idle animals. It is an infallible rule that the grain ration should be halved during periods of idleness.

THE DOTTED LINES INDICATE NORMAL SIZE.

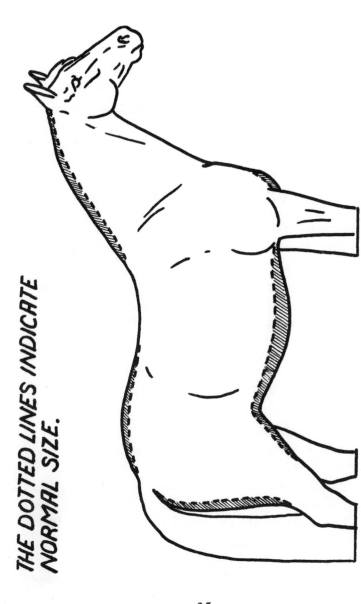

OBESITY IN HORSES IS NOT ATTRACTIVE OR HEALTHY.

Feeding Special Cases

GREEDY EATERS

Horses that bolt their grain should have it spread out thinly over a large area so that they cannot get large mouthfuls. Chopped hay added to the grain will also force the animal to eat slower. A few chunks of block salt or rocks, baseball size, placed in the food box will slow down a greedy eater.

HORSES THAT STOCK

Horses that stock should have their feed ration very carefully regulated according to the work they do. If idle, even for short periods, their ration should be proportionately decreased. Long periods of idleness are not good for such horses. There should always be enough exercise given them to keep the circulation of limbs active.

THIN HORSES

When feeding a thin but otherwise healthy animal, take into consideration the fact that the weakness of the muscles of his limbs is also reflected in the muscles of his stomach and bowels. Until a thin animal gains strength, he is not capable of digesting large amounts of food without incurring the risk of indigestion or colic. In such cases, small amounts of food should be given often. As the animal grows stronger the quantity of each feed may be increased. Plenty of fresh water is also important in the restoration of thin horses.

Changing The Diet

Whenever a change is made in the amount or type of feed, take at least several days in making the change to avoid upsetting the horse's digestive system. Drastic changes, such as changing from a regular hay–grain diet to a complete pelleted one, should be made gradually over a period of two weeks. Any sudden change in a horse's diet will almost always result in colic.

The Feeding Schedule

An irregular feeding schedule can cause mild to serious colic in some horses, especially those who are confined and are unable to satisfy their hunger by grazing. To avoid possible upsets, feed at the same times every day. If it is not always possible for you to be present at feeding time, make arrangements with a dependable person to feed for you. Impatient horses will often develop a habit of pawing or kicking when meals are late. These actions could lead to costly repairs or an injured horse.

WHEN HORSES ARE WORKING HARD, IT SHOULD BE KEPT IN MIND THAT THE CONCENTRATES SUPPLY THE ENERGY FOR MUSCULAR WORK. IF NOT ENOUGH GRAIN IS FED THE ANIMAL, BODY FAT MUST SUPPLY THE ENERGY. AFTER THE BODY FAT IS EXHAUSTED, THE MUSCLES OR OTHER PROTEIN TISSUES MUST SUPPLY THE ENERGY, AND THE RESULTS WILL BE A THIN HORSE.

Concentrates

Feeds are divided into several categories and one of these basic groupings is concerned with fiber content and total digestible nutrients. These indicate the energy values of feeds. Concentrates are defined as feeds low in fiber and high in nutrients. Various grains and high-grade products, such as wheat bran, linseed meal and cottonseed meal feed, fall in this class.

Oats

No grain is so keenly relished by horses as oats. Oats are also the safest of all grains for the horse because the adherent hull affords enough bulk to prevent many errors in feeding that are common when more concentrated grains are used.

Oats may be fed whole or crushed, although crushed oats insure more thorough mastication and digestion. Oats, fed with timothy or a good grass hay, offer enough protein to provide a balanced ration for most mature horses.

Barley

Barley is good for horses and it is quite often substituted for oats. It is higher in protein and supplies more total digestive nutrients than oats. Barley, because it is much heavier than oats, should be mixed with ground oats, wheat bran, or chopped hay to avert the danger of colic.

Corn

Corn, though low in protein, ranks high in both nutrients and net energy. It is rich in nitrogen-free extract which is nearly all starch and is also higher in fat than any other cereal except oats.

Corn is so highly concentrated that care must be taken not to over-feed it to horses in the summer. Corn will also tend toward excessive fat. Ear corn keeps better than that shelled and since it takes longer to chew, it will be more thoroughly masticated. Cobs ground with corn provide the needed bulk.

Wheat Bran

Wheat bran possesses four qualities that make it a valuable adjunct to the horse's ration, namely: its palatability, nutritive bulk and mild laxative action. It has a higher protein content than corn and ranks only slightly below oats in nutrients.

Bran may be fed dry or as a mash. Used dry, it is good for mixing with grain to induce slower eating and more thorough mastication. An occasional bran mash is beneficial. In this form it has a more pronounced laxative action.

Molasses

Molasses is a good appetizer and conditioner. It has a mild laxative effect and reduces dustiness of some coarse feed mixtures. Although a source of energy, molasses should not exceed more than 10% of the concentrate ration.

Linseed Meal

Linseed meal is an excellent feeding supplement for horses that are in run-down condition. It has a slight laxative action and its use will improve the coat. Linseed meal is rich in protein and has a strong taste appeal, but fed in excessive amounts, it can cause digestive problems.

Cottonseed Meal

Cottonseed meal is often used as a protein supplement in rations for horses. It will improve the animal's condition and appearance, but the use of large amounts can cause digestive disturbances. It is not particularly relished by most horses and therefore should be mixed with better-liked feeds, such as oats and bran.

Commercial Horse Feed

Most commercial horse feeds provide a balanced ration. Basically, they are combinations of grains and grain by-products, proteins, minerals and vitamins. They are very convenient to use and store, but don't rely entirely on them for growing horses or lactating mares. These animals will normally need more protein than most commercial feeds supply. The commercial feeds usually identify their protein content, quantities of fat, fiber and minerals. Carefully select the one best suited for your horse's needs.

AS A SOURCE OF PROTEIN FOR HORSES,
DEHYDRATED ALFALFA PELLETS ARE
HIGHLY RECOMMENDED. FOR EXTRA
VALUE THEY ALSO HAVE MANY NU-
TRITIONAL PROPERTIES NOT FOUND
IN ANY OTHER PROTEINS AND THEY
OFFER TWICE AS MUCH VITAMIN A AS
CARROTS.

Weights Of Concentrates

In calculating rations for the horse it is often necessary to use weights rather than measures. In practical feeding operations it is usually more convenient to measure the concentrates. The tabulation shown below will serve as a guide for those who feed by measure.

CONCENTRATE	APPROXIMATE POUNDS PER QUART
Oats	1.0
Oats (ground)	0.7
Barley	1.5
Corn (cracked)	1.6
Corn (shelled)	1.8
Molasses Feed	0.8
Wheat Bran	0.8
Linseed Meal	0.9
Cottonseed Meal	1.5

THE COFFEE CAN DIPPER

A two-pound coffee can is a favorite "dipper" used by horsemen for concentrates. The horseowner knows that the container once held two pounds of coffee, but it should be remembered that concentrates weigh differently than coffee. In most cases a two-pound coffee can will hold more, or less, than two pounds of a concentrate.

Complete Pelleted Feed

The new hay-grain pelleted horse feed is convenient and makes a minimum demand for storage. It will also save buying and storing extras as most pelleted feeds contain measured amounts of vitamins, minerals and salt. Consider comparative costs and it may be found that a complete pelleted ration is quite reasonable, especially when hay prices are high.

It has been found that old horses and those with heaves caused by hay dust allergies will, in most cases, do much better on a complete pelleted ration.

One possible disadvantage of a complete pelleted ration is that because it offers so little bulk, some horses will turn to chewing on stalls and fences. A small amount of hay fed to confined animals will keep them happy.

There are many brands and types of pelleted rations available. Some offer more grain than hay, while others offer more hay than grain. Read the labels carefully and choose the one best suited to your horse's needs.

Shown on the next page are two different complete pelleted horse rations. The top one, with a 13% protein level, would be suggested for young animals doing light to moderate work. The lower one, with only a 10% protein level, would be better suited for older horses or those who are idle.

Pelleted Horse Ration

	net weight 100 pounds
Crude Protein, not less than	13.00%
Crude Fat, not less than	2.00%
Crude Fiber, not more than	18.00%
Crude Ash, not more than	9.00%
Added Minerals, not more than	2.00%

Choice chopped alfalfa hay, chopped oat hay, gr. barley, milrun, gr. heavy white oats, gr. milo, cane molasses with phosphoric acid, soyo bean meal, linseed meal, def. phosphate, salt, premix added: rice mill by-products (not to exceed ½%), corn distiller's dried grains with solubles, starch, ascorbic acid 50 gm. per ton, vitamin A palmitate with D-activated animal sterol (source of vitamin D 3) dl-alpha-tocopheryl acetate, (source of vitamin E) vitamin B-12 supplement, niacin, calcium pantothenate, folic acid, thiamine mononitrate, manganous oxide, zinc oxide, iron carbonate, copper oxide, calcium iodate, cobalt carbonate.

Pelleted Horse Ration

	net weight 100 pounds
Crude Protein, not less than	10.00%
Crude Fat, not less than	1.00%
Crude Fiber, not more than	30.00%
Ash, not more than	8.00%
Added Minerals, not more than	1.50%

Choice chopped alfalfa hay, chopped oat hay, rice millfeed, max. 15%, cane molasses with phosphoric acid, salt, Premix added: rice mill by-product (not to exceed ½%) corn distiller's dried grains with solubles, starch, ascorbic acid 50 gm. per ton, vitamin A palmitate with D-activated animal sterol (source of vitamin D3), dl-alpha-tocopheryl acetate source of vitamin E), Vitamin B-12 supplement, riboflavin supplement, niacin, calcium pantothenate, folic acid, thiamine mononitrate, manganous oxide, zinc oxide, iron carbonate, copper oxide, calcium iodate, cobalt carbonate.

Roughage

Hay provides the roughage which is very important in the horse's diet. Hay or other bulky feed is an absolute necessity if the horse is to digest his feed properly. No horse can remain healthy if fed grain alone, irrespective of the amount fed.

Good quality hay offers bulk plus energy, protein, minerals, carotene and several of the B Vitamins. It should be made from plants cut at an early stage of maturity and cured so that it is leafy and green. Hay that is moldy, musty or dusty should always be avoided.

Alfalfa

The excellence of alfalfa hay is due to its high yield, its palatability, its richness in protein, its unusually high content of calcium and its value as a source of Vitamin A and D. It has a nutritive ratio which more closely approximates that of grains than do the common roughages.

The amount of alfalfa should be limited as it has a stimulating effect on heat production and body metabolism, therefore it is considered less desirable for feeding during hot weather. Because excessive amounts may also lead to digestive ailments, it is agreed by many that alfalfa should not comprise more than one half of the hay allowance.

Timothy

Timothy, long recognized as the standard hay for feeding horses, is usually freer of dust and mold than legume hay. It is low in protein and minerals and these should be otherwise supplemented when feeding timothy to growing animals and broodmares.

Red Clover

Red clover is often grown in combination with timothy and it is second only to alfalfa in food values. Cut at the proper stage of maturity, it has about two-thirds as much digestible protein as alfalfa, but furnishes more total digestible nutrients.

Grain Hay

Grain hay is made from the cereal grasses such as oats, barley and wheat. It has a feed total value approximately equivalent to other feeding hays, but is somewhat richer in protein. Grain hays are relished by horses and highly considered by horse owners in the areas in which they are produced. Grain hay should be cut while the grain is in the milk or early-dough stage, as at this stage most of the nutrients are still in the leaves and stems rather than concentrated in the grain. Grain hay seldom is as green in color as other types of hay and is often mistaken for straw by those not familiar with it.

Grass Hay

Grass hay is made from any of the cultivated grasses or wild grasses which have feeding value. Such grass hays include redtop, orchard grass, Bermuda grass, Kentucky bluegrass and ryegrass. Good grass hay is generally the equivalent of other feeding hays.

CARROTS, WHICH ARE RICH IN VITAMIN A, ARE RELISHED BY HORSES. A POUND A DAY WILL HAVE A BENEFICIAL EFFECT, ESPECIALLY WHEN GREEN FEED IS NOT AVAILABLE.

Green Roughage

Fresh green feed is truly the natural diet of the horse and in most cases, the domesticated horse receives too little of this kind of food. Although it has been proven that green feed is not absolutely essential, it is desirable when properly supplied.

When horses are first allowed to graze, especially on new spring grass, they should be allowed only a short time the first day. Gradually increase the time from day to day. Green grass is a laxative and unless judiciously used will cause diarrhea. Special care should be exercised with legumes, especially if they are wet or have been touched by frost, as they are likely to cause colic.

Stall feeding of limited amounts of freshly cut green roughage is sometimes practiced when horses cannot be pastured. When feeding fresh cut grasses, great care must be exercised to see that fermentation or spoilage has not commenced. It is always safest to feed only the freshly cut grasses, and in small amounts.

TO PROVIDE HEALTH FOR THE HORSE AND ECONOMY FOR THE HORSE OWNER, PASTURE SHOULD BE RELIED ON AS MUCH AS IT IS POSSIBLE. RICH GREEN FORAGE IS THE BEST AND MOST NATURAL FOOD FOR HORSES. PASTURE ALSO PROVIDES AN ABUNDANCE OF IMPORTANT VITAMINS AND MINERALS.

Pasture

In addition to providing minerals, vitamins and other nutrients, pasturing also provides exercise on natural footing with plenty of sun, fresh air and lowered feeding costs as added virtues. Although pasturing is the ideal existence for horses, it may have some laxative effects and produce a greater tendency to sweat.

The mature horse, ridden only a few times a week for short periods, may be adequately fed on good green pasture from rich soil. Growing animals may require a phosphorous supplement for proper bone development because while grass is high in calcium it is low in phosphorous.

The ideal horse pasture should provide fresh water, salt and shade. The land should be well drained to eliminate any possible breeding place for mosquitoes. It should be free of holes, stumps, pipe, wire and any other hazards. The pasture should be fertilized periodically to maintain longer growing periods and produce richer feed. A system of alternate grazing should be used to prevent depleting the vigor of plants.

BARBED WIRE SHOULD NEVER BE USED FOR HORSE PASTURES.

Pasture Supplement

When the horse pasture turns brown from drought or a freeze, it means the vitamins are no longer being provided. Extra feed, especially that with Vitamin A and protein, will be required. A supplement block, described below, is often used and will usually provide the required extras. These blocks, resembling a 50 pound salt block, are placed out in the pasture where the horse will have free choice of the supplement.

Pasture Supplement Block

Crude protein not less than 12.5%
Crude fat not less than 2.0%
Crude fiber not more than 8.0%
Calcium not less than 1.5%
Calcium not more than 2.5%
Phosphorus not less than 0.5%
Iodine not less than 0.0003%
Salt not less than 12.5%
Salt not more than 15.0%

Ingredients

Ground yellow corn and/or ground grain sorghums, soybean meal and/or cottonseed meal and/or linseed meal, cane molasses and/or beet molasses and/or corn sugar molasses and/or grain sorghums sugar molasses, wheat middlings, alfalfa meal, dehydrated alfalfa meal, preserved with ethoxyquin, vitamin A supplement, low fluorine rock phosphate, calcium carbonate, iodized salt, iron oxide, manganese sulfate, manganese oxide, copper oxide, cobalt carbonate, zinc oxide.

51

SUPPLEMENTS AND
CONDITIONERS
FOR HORSES

Supplements And Conditioners

In recent years people have become extremely vitamin-conscious and as a result the market has become flooded with special supplements and conditioners for both man and beast. The high potency conditioners and ration balancers for horses are usually expensive and in some cases they could do more harm than good. For example, a supplement very rich in protein could cause founder in an older horse that is idle most of the time. On the other hand, these same conditioners are often recommended for stallions in heavy service, animals recovering from illness, sick animals, pregnant mares and growing animals.

Keep in mind that the mature, healthy horse, fed a good balanced ration, will rarely require a conditioner or vitamin supplement.

IT SHOULD ALWAYS BE REMEMBERED THAT NO TWO HORSES CAN BE FED EXACTLY ALIKE WITH THE SAME RESULTS. DIFFERENCES IN METABOLISM WILL PREVENT ANY TWO HORSES FROM DOING EQUALLY WELL ON THE SAME RATION. SOME HORSES REQUIRE MORE FEED THAN OTHERS AND A DIFFERENT KIND OF CARE.

The Feed Allowance

The eyes of the horse owner must regulate the amount of food given to each individual horse. Each horse differs from another in food habits and tendency to put on weight. Moreover, the age and degree of activity of horses are quite important factors.

A good rule of thumb is: for an average horse doing light to moderate work, feed one pound of grain for each hundred pounds of horse. (Idle horses should have less.) A suggested ration allowance for a mature horse doing light to moderate work is four pounds of oats, one pound of barley and seven pounds of mixed hay—timothy and clover or alfalfa and grass hay. This is for one feeding. This ration, fed morning and night, provides the horse with 10 pounds of grain and 14 pounds of hay daily. In addition, water, salt and minerals should be provided.

If this ration should cause the horse to gain weight, reduce the oats and increase the hay slightly. If the horse should lose weight, reverse the process: more grain and less hay.

THE NEW 18-QUART POLYETHYLENE CORNER FEEDERS ARE EASILY INSTALLED IN ANY STABLE OR CORRAL.

A GALVANIZED TUB FASTENED WITH TWO SNAPS ALSO MAKES AN IDEAL CONTAINER FOR FEEDING CONCENTRATES.

Feeding Equipment

The horse's ration should never be thrown on the ground. This is especially important in areas where the soil is sandy. Sand picked up with the food can cause irritation of the intestines and also lead to impaction.

Grain containers may range from very simple, inexpensive boxes to elaborate and costly ones. Regardless of the type, the grain container should be kept clean. This is especially important after feeding a bran mash or ration mixed with molasses.

Horsemen differ as to the advisability of using a hay rack in the stable. Feeding from the floor has the advantage of reducing construction cost and prevents any possible injury to the horse. But a careful allotment of hay will be required in order to prevent waste. Some horses acquire the habit of pawing the hay and this will usually result in wasted hay or the animal eating contaminated hay. The use of a hay rack in a dirt corral is always advisable.

Always feed the horse in a normal position, which is shoulder level or lower. It's easier for the animal to eat and the hay dust will not irritate his eyes or lungs.

THE COLOSTRUM IS A MILK SECRETED BY THE MARE FOR THE FIRST FEW DAYS AFTER FOALING. IT DIFFERS FROM ORDINARY MILK. IT IS MORE CONCENTRATED, HIGHER IN PROTEIN, RICHER IN VITAMIN A, CONTAINS MORE ANTIBODIES AND HAS A STIMULATING EFFECT ON THE ALIMENTARY TRACT. IT IS VERY IMPORTANT THAT THE NEWBORN FOAL SECURES THIS MILK.

Feeding The Broodmare

In comparison to geldings and unbred mares, the gestating–lactating broodmare must be fed differently. She will require a greater quantity of food, more proteins, vitamins and minerals. Dusty, moldy or frozen feeds, which are avoided for all horses, must be especially avoided for the broodmare. Such feeds may cause abortion.

Once a mare is in foal she is obviously under the double burden of maintaining both herself and the foal-to-be which grows more demanding all the time. If the mare's diet is lacking in any essential element, it will be drawn from her system by the foal, thus depleting her own supply. A full, rich diet results in a healthy mare, a healthy foal and rich, nourishing milk.

During the first half of her pregnancy, the mare should be provided with top quality roughage, at least two pounds of grain a day and all the necessary vitamins and minerals. After the sixth month, the idle mare should have one pound of oats, one pound of cracked corn and supplements, along with about 15 pounds of grass-legume hay.

After the mare has foaled, withhold all grain for two days. For the first 24 hours feed only a little hay and a limited amount of water from which the chill has been taken. A light feed of wet bran mash is suggested for the first feed after foaling. A reasonable amount of hay is allowed after the first day, but the grain ration should be kept light for about 10 days after foaling. Too much grain too soon after foaling may produce digestive disturbances in the mare or cause her to produce too much milk, which is liable to cause indigestion in the foal.

If it is possible for the mare to foal on clean, lush pasture, she will normally regulate her own feed needs.

Lactation, or milk production, is more of a strain on the mare than pregnancy and she will now require almost twice as much digestible nutrients. About three weeks after foaling start increasing the grain ration until she is getting six pounds of oats, four pounds of cracked corn and one pound of dehydrated alfalfa pellets a day. The hay ration should be maintained at 15 pounds daily. If the mare is on good lush green pasture, only about one-half of the grain and hay ration will be required.

THE PROPER AGE TO WEAN A FOAL WITH SAFETY IS FROM 4 TO 7 MONTHS. THE SEPARATION OF MARE AND FOAL SHOULD BE DONE GRADUALLY.

SIDE VIEW

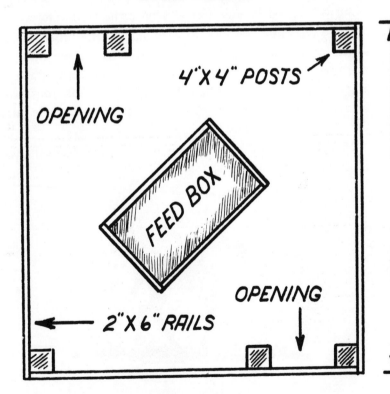

4"X 4" POSTS

OPENING

FEED BOX

OPENING

2"X 6" RAILS

TOP VIEW

DIAGRAM OF A CREEP FEEDER

Feeding The Foal

A foal makes the greatest growth of his life during the first 18 months and the food he gets at this time is especially important. A foal stunted in early life by insufficient food cannot properly develop later in life.

In order to promote early development and avoid a setback at weaning time, it is important to encourage a foal to eat supplementary feed as early as possible. For this purpose a creep feeder should be provided. A good basic ration of crushed oats and bran should be placed in the feeder along with good legume hay as soon as he is able to eat it.

After weaning, add ground corn and a little linseed meal to the creep feed. Some horsemen also feed cow's milk at this time or add powdered milk to the creep feed to assure a good supply of protein, calcium and phosphorous. Increase the hay ration to about 10 pounds a day. Be sure the hay is high in nutrients.

Plenty of fresh air, sun, fresh water and exercise is also important to the growing foal.

The Orphan Foal

If the mare should die before the foal is able to get her colostrum, a veterinarian can provide a substitute by injection. Then, with care, the foal can be raised on cow's milk.

A formula of one pint of milk, one-quarter pint of limewater and one teaspoon of sugar will provide two feedings at the start. Be sure to warm the formula before offering it to the foal. Feed it to the foal in an ordinary nursing bottle. For the first week, feed the foal every hour. If the foal progresses satisfactorily, gradually increase the amount of formula and lengthen the periods of formula and lengthen the periods between feedings. From 8 to 14 days feed one pint every two hours and start using whole milk instead of the formula. A suckle pail should also replace the bottle. From 15 days to 21 days feed one quart every four hours and during this time begin to encourage the foal to eat a ration of crushed oats, bran and a little linseed meal. At 6 weeks, gradually substitute sweet skim milk for the whole milk and at three months reduce the milk feedings to three times a day, but allow the foal all he will drink each time.

Feeding The Stallion

The feeding program throughout the year should be such as to keep the stallion vigorous and thrifty at all times. Just before the breeding season, the feed ration should be increased. The quantity of grain fed will vary with the individual stallion, the exercise provided, services allowed and the quality of hay.

During the breeding season, the stallion's ration should contain more proteins and additional vitamins and minerals, but the ration should be carefully regulated to prevent the stallion from gaining too much weight. A fat condition can lead to infertility. During the balance of the year a stallion may be fed like other horses similarly handled.

TODAY'S PLEASURE HORSES ARE NOT THE EASIEST HORSES TO FEED BECAUSE THEIR USE IS OFTEN SO IRREGULAR. MOST OF THE WEEK THEY ARE IDLE... THEN SUDDENLY WORKED HARD OVER THE WEEKEND. A DAILY EXERCISE PERIOD WOULD HELP KEEP THE HORSE IN CONDITION FOR THE WEEK-END AND ALSO HELP IN THE FEEDING PROGRAM.

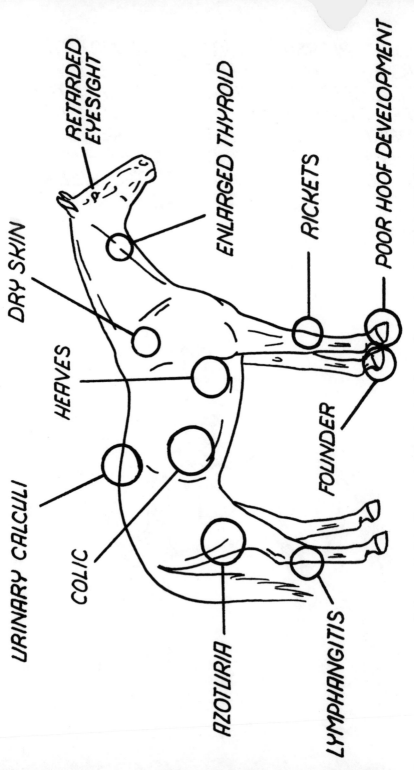

DISORDERS CAUSED BY IMPROPER FEEDING

RETARDED EYESIGHT

ENLARGED THYROID

RICKETS

POOR HOOF DEVELOPMENT

DRY SKIN

HEAVES

FOUNDER

URINARY CALCULI

COLIC

AZOTURIA

LYMPHANGITIS

Nutritional Diseases

The diseases to be described are all serious and the sad part is that they are all caused by mistakes in feeding the horse. Be constantly aware of the consequences of careless feeding. Spare your horse from paying the penalty for human error.

COLIC

Colic is one of the most common problems among horses and could almost always be avoided by proper feeding and handling. Colic pain in the horse is a symptom of disease or conditions affecting the stomach, intestines and any other organ within the abdomen.

A horse with colic will suffer great pain. His abdomen may be distended and considerable stomach rumbling may be heard. The animal refuses food and becomes restless. He paws, bites at his sides and groans. Breathing becomes labored.

If colic is not relieved, one disturbance may lead to another. The discontinued muscular movements of the intestines may result in gas fermentation, extreme constipation, catarrh edema and hemorrhages. Severe colic may lead to a ruptured stomach or intestine, intestinal gangrene or abdominal cavity infection, and result in death.

At the first symptoms of colic, withhold all food. Walk the animal quietly until the vet arrives. Never allow a horse with colic to roll or thrash about.

A HORSE WITH COLIC SHOULD NEVER BE MADE TO RUN OR ALLOWED TO ROLL VIOLENTLY. SUCH ACTIONS COULD CAUSE THE RUPTURE OF AN INTERNAL ORGAN AND RESULT IN THE ANIMAL'S DEATH.

AZOTURIA

This disease usually affects the highly fed horses. It strikes without warning and any or all of the leg muscles may be affected. It is most common in the hind legs and the large muscles of the loin and hindquarters. They become hard, stiff and painful to any pressure. The horse's movements become uncoordinated and muscles tremble. The breakdown of muscle tissue releases pigments into the blood stream which work their way into the urine and cause it to become very dark. Advanced cases may result in a complete kidney failure.

Horses which have suffered this disease and recovered are predisposed to further attacks and, therefore, they must be fed lightly on grain and be exercised frequently.

A HORSE SUFFERING WITH AZOTURIA

HEAVES

Heaves occur more often in horses which are fed dusty roughage and grains or large amounts of dry roughage containing little nourishment. Confinement in poorly ventilated stables and repeated work which causes severe effort in breathing also contribute to the disease.

When heaves develop in a horse, breathing becomes difficult because tiny air sacs in the lungs have lost their elasticity. Breathing "in" becomes short and expiration difficult. There is a noticeable rolling forward of the ribs under the skin which eventually causes a groove in the back of the ribs known as the "heave line." Eventually a large barrel chest is developed which causes the ribs to spring apart and the diaphragm muscles to become enlarged. The animal will have no stamina and usually becomes unthrifty. There is no cure for heaves but special rations for horses suffering with the disease are available.

URINARY CALCULI

Urinary calculi is a disorder of the kidney and urinary tract in which stones, or calculi, develop and block the passage of urine. A horse with this disease makes frequent attempts to urinate, the results being scanty. There is noted restlessness and the animal will walk with a straddling gait. Chronic obstruction may result in rupture of the bladder. Suggested causes of this disease are shortages of Vitamin A and D, an imbalance of calcium, phosphorous and other minerals.

VITAMIN A DEFICIENCY

Vitamin A deficiency may reduce the ability to see in dim light and in prolonged cases permanent blindness may result. The skin of the horse may become dry and scaly and the coat rough. Reproductive disturbances may occur, along with respiratory ailments. The hoof development is poor and the hoofs are rough and more liable to chip and crack. Limited amounts of forage or feeds that have been stored so long that their natural carotene has been lost, may cause Vitamin A deficiency.

RICKETS

Rickets is a disease usually found in young animals. The bones of affected animals do not grow or harden properly. The legs and ribs are most affected. The knee and hock joints are enlarged and painful to move. In advanced cases the animal may lie down more than normal and weakened bones may cause the legs to bow. Early warning of rickets are loss of appetite, weight loss, digestive disturbances and convulsions marked by rigid muscles and stiff legs.

Adequate amounts of calcium, phosphorous and Vitamin D will normally prevent rickets.

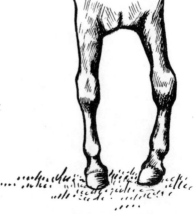

ICKETS IN A FOAL'S
RONT LEGS.

THE RINGS ASSOCIATED WITH CHRONIC FOUNDER ARE CLOSE TOGETHER AT THE TOE AND FAR APART AT THE HEEL. THESE RINGS SHOULD NOT BE CONFUSED WITH SLIGHT RIDGES WHICH MAY RESULT FROM STOMACH DISORDERS.

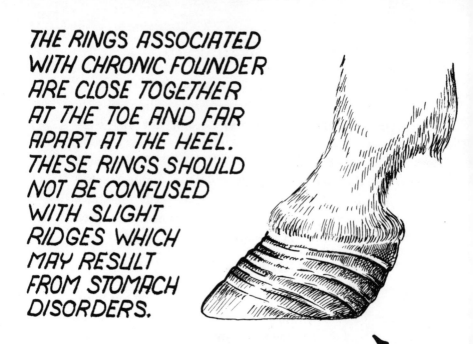

A FOUNDERED FOOT
(LAMINITIS)

NORMAL FOOT   FOUNDERED FOOT

LAMINITIS

Overfeeding of grain, feeding spoiled feed or allowing excessive amounts of water to an overheated horse will all contribute to laminitis or foundered foot. A horse stricken with this disorder will appear suddenly lame in the fore feet. The front feet are placed well forward and the horse rocks back on his hind feet. The affected feet are hot. The pulse and respiration are considerably accelerated. The animal can move only with great pain and difficulty.

If early recovery does not occur, permanent changes develop in the foot. Feet that have been affected with laminitis often remain hypersensitive and the slightest pressure on the sole evokes pain and lameness.

LYMPHANGITIS

Failure to reduce the grain ration of a well-conditioned horse during periods of idleness is a major cause of lymphangitis. The disease is characterized by marked swelling, heat, tenderness and lameness in one or both hind legs. There is a loss of appetite, rapid pulse and high temperature. The affected leg may swell to twice its normal size and the skin may become moist with exuding serum. Recovery is seldom complete. A permanently enlarged leg may result.

A CASE OF LYMPHANGITIS.

A BRAN MASH FED ONCE A WEEK IS VERY BENEFICIAL. TAKE ABOUT 3 QUARTS OF BRAN, ADD SOME SALT AND THEN ENOUGH BOILING WATER TO WET THOROUGHLY. COVER AND ALLOW TO STEAM UNTIL COOL. OATS MAY BE ADDED TO THE COOLED MASH TO MAKE IT MORE PALATABLE.

EPSOM SALTS ARE VALUABLE FOR REGULATING THE CONDITION OF THE BOWELS. A FULL DOSE OF ½ POUND ACTS AS A PURGATIVE. A ¼ POUND MAY BE GIVEN TO IDLE HORSES ONCE A WEEK.

Defecation

The manure, or droppings, are often a good indication of the condition of the digestive tract. An examination may reveal the following irregularities:

1. Hard droppings may indicate a lack of water, a lack of exercise, dry or indigestible food.
2. Very soft droppings may indicate too much hard work, fatigue, too much fresh green or alfalfa, excessive use of bran or irritation of the intestines.
3. Slimy or mucus-covered droppings, or those having an offensive odor, indicate too highly concentrated feed.
4. Unmasticated grain indicates that the teeth may be sharp or diseased, or that the animal eats too fast.

Normal droppings should be fairly well formed but soft enough to flatten when dropped. Droppings should be free from offensive odor or mucus slime. The color will vary from yellow to green, according to the nature of the feed. It should not be filled with grains that are either wholly or partially unmasticated. Normal defecation occurs 8 to 10 times in 24 hours.

DIARRHEA

Diarrhea is not necessarily a symptom of disease, as it may be an effort to dislodge indigestible matter, but if the condition persists, the animal loses flesh and his appetite. Persistent diarrhea may indicate an error of the diet or physical disorder.

The Teeth

Improper mastication of food caused by tooth problems may lead to indigestion, malnutrition and even general weakness and emaciation. Any tooth irregularities should be corrected as soon as possible by a veterinarian.

On the whole, a horse's teeth keep quite sound and decay (such as occurs in human teeth) is uncommon. On the other hand, owing to the fact that the horse's upper jaw is somewhat wider than the lower, and that, from the fact of the teeth not being properly apposed, a sharp ridge is often left unworn on the inside of the lower molars and on the outside of the uppers. This condition may excoriate the tongue and cheeks to a considerable extent. Sharp teeth may be indicated by slobbering, holding the head to one side while eating, reluctance to eat and loss of weight.

The teeth are usually changing about the same time that a colt is being trained or broken. It is at this time that the temporary molars of some colts fail to shed and become caps on the crowns of the emerging permanent molars. In such cases the animal will experience considerable pain, discomfort and weight loss.

THE INCISORS OF
AN OLD HORSE. $\longrightarrow$

A more frequent disorder is alveolar periostitis, which is usually caused by food particles or infectious materials working their way into spaces in the jawbone. Infection enters the dental pulp from the grinding molars. Eventually there will be an offensive odor and chewing becomes painful and difficult. Abscesses may form deep in the sockets and as the blood supply becomes obstructed, desiccation and splitting teeth may occur.

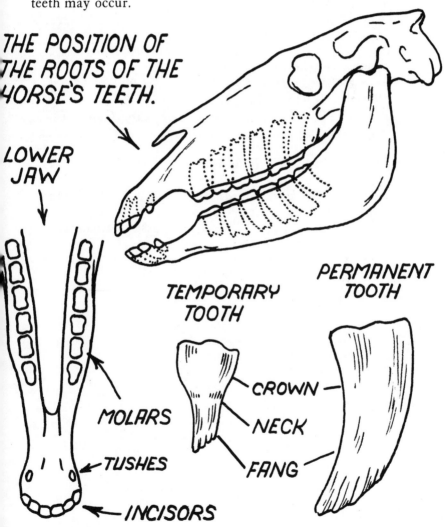

THE POSITION OF THE ROOTS OF THE HORSE'S TEETH.

LOWER JAW

TEMPORARY TOOTH

PERMANENT TOOTH

CROWN

NECK

FANG

MOLARS

TUSHES

INCISORS

Bibliography

BOOKS

Ensminger, M. E. *Horse Husbandry.* Illinois: Interstate Printers & Publishers, 1951.

Hayes, Captain M. Horace. *Veterinary Notes for Horse Owners.* New York: Arco Publishing Co., 1970.

Lyon, Col. W. E. *First Aid Hints for the Horse Owner.* London: Collins, 1951.

Miller, Robert D. *Health Problems of the Horse.* Colorado: Western Horseman Inc., 1967.

Simmons, Hoyt H. *Horseman's Veterinary Guide.* Colorado: Western Horseman Inc., 1963.

BOOKLETS

Know Practical Horse Feeding. Nebraska: Farnam Horse Library, no date.

Know the Anatomy of the Horse. Nebraska: Farnam Horse Library, 1971.